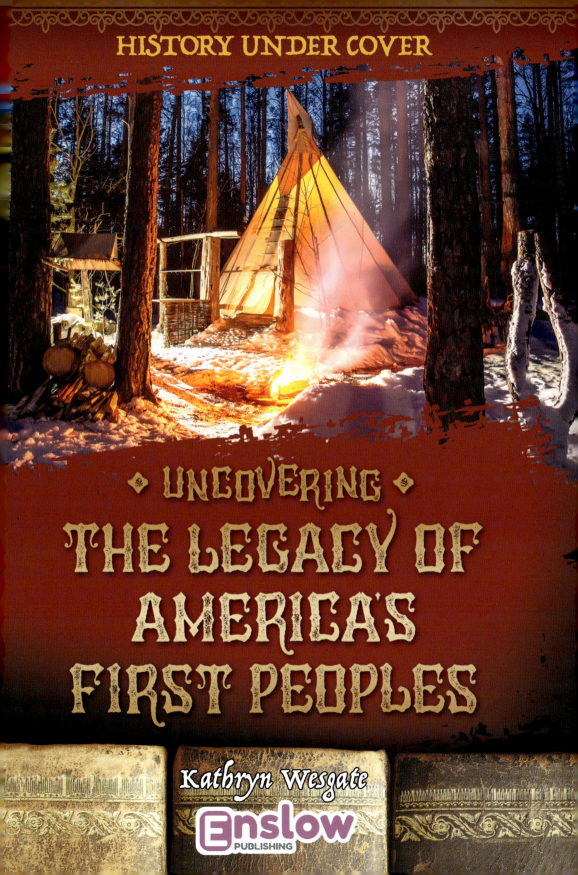

Please visit our website, www.enslow.com. For a free color catalog of all our high-quality books, call toll free 1-800-398-2504 or fax 1-877-980-4454.

Cataloging-in-Publication Data

Names: Wesgate, Kathryn.
Title: Uncovering the legacy of America's first peoples / Kathryn Wesgate.
Description: New York : Enslow Publishing, 2023. | Series: History under cover | Includes glossary and index.
Identifiers: ISBN 9781978528949 (pbk.) | ISBN 9781978528963 (library bound) | ISBN 9781978528956 (6pack) | ISBN 9781978528970 (ebook)
Subjects: LCSH: Indians of North America–Juvenile literature. | Indians of North America–History–Juvenile literature.
Classification: LCC E77.4 W4226 2023 | DDC 973.04'97–dc23

Published in 2023 by
Enslow Publishing
29 East 21st Street
New York, NY 10010

Copyright © 2023 Enslow Publishing

Portions of this work were originally authored by Janey Levy and published as *North America's First People*. All new material this edition authored by Kathryn Wesgate.

Designer: Leslie Taylor
Editor: Kate Mikoley

Photo credits: Photo credits: Cover, FOTOGRIN/Shutterstock.com; series art (scrolls) Magenta10/Shutterstock.com, series art (back cover leather texture) levan828/Shutterstock.com; series art (front cover books) RMMPPhotography/Shutterstock.com; series art (title font) MagicPics/Shutterstock.com; series art (ripped inside pgs) kaczor58/Shutterstock.com; p. 4 GAS-photo/Shutterstock.com; p. 5 (cave bear) Daniel Eskridge/Shutterstock.com; p. 5 (saber-toothed cat) Daniel Eskridge/Shutterstock.com; p. 5 (giant sloth) Aunt Spray/Shutterstock.com; p. 6 SurfsUp/Shutterstock.com; p. 7 Microgen/Shutterstock.com; p. 7 (map) Sunny Whale/Shutterstock.com; p. 8 Denis Simonov/Shutterstock.com; p. 9 https://commons.wikimedia.org/wiki/File:Clovis_Rummells_Maske.jpg; p. 10 Daniel Eskridge/Shutterstock.com; p. 11 Chad Love/APImages.com; p. 12 & 13 Jeff Barnard/APimages.com; p. 15 (inset) Gorodenkoff/Shutterstock.com; p. 15 (map) Bardocz Peter/Shutterstock.com p. 16 & 19 https://commons.wikimedia.org/wiki/File:Kennewick_Man.jpg; p. 17 Emmanuel Laurent/ScienceSource.com; p. 17 (top) J.D.S/Shutterstock.com; p. 18 https://www.loc.gov/pictures/item/2003668230/; p. 19 Emmanuel Laurent/ScienceSource.com; p. 20 Peter Hermes Furian/Shutterstock.com; p. 21 Esteban De Armas/Shutterstock.com; p. 22 Linda Szeto/Shutterstock.com; p. 23 Tom Silver/Shutterstock.com; p. 23 (hare) Egoreichenkov Evgenii/Shutterstock.com; p. 24 Pyty/Shutterstock.com; p. 25 (left) https://commons.wikimedia.org/wiki/File:Clovis_Point.jpg p. 25 (right) hmountainpix/Shutterstock.com; p 26 (map) titoOnz/Shutterstock.com; p. 26 (koala) Yatra/Shutterstock.com; p. 27 Jens Dresling/APImages.com; p. 28 Gorodenkoff/Shutterstock.com; p. 29 Microgen/Shutterstock.com.

All rights reserved. No part of this book may be reproduced in any form without permission in writing from the publisher, except by a reviewer.

Printed in the United States of America

Some of the images in this book illustrate individuals who are models. The depictions do not imply actual situations or events.

CPSIA compliance information: Batch #CSENS23: For further information, contact Enslow Publishing, New York, New York, at 1-800-398-2504.

Find us on

A Startling Discovery	4
Searching for the First Americans	6
The People of Clovis	8
Paisley Caves Discoveries	12
Even Earlier People?	14
Stumbling Across a Skull	16
Making the Way to America	20
Crossing the Atlantic?	24
Recent Discoveries	26
Glossary	30
For More Information	31
Index	32

Words in the glossary appear in bold or highlighted type the first time they are used in the text.

A Startling Discovery

A group of divers made a startling but extraordinary discovery in 2007. While mapping an underwater Mexican cave system, they found a teenage girl's skeleton. It rested among the remains of animals from the last **ice age**. At 12,000 to 13,000 years old, it was the oldest complete human skeleton found in the Americas.

The skeleton yielded **DNA**, which helped solve a long-standing riddle: Why don't the earliest Americans' skulls resemble those of modern Native Americans? Did the two groups migrate from different places or at different times? The DNA showed the ancient Americans were indeed ancestors of modern Native Americans. The dissimilarities weren't the result of different migrations, but simply changes over time. While the discovery solved at least one mystery, much about America's first peoples remains unknown.

The animals whose remains were found with Naia included extinct creatures such as cave bears, saber-toothed cats, and giant ground sloths.

~ A Deadly Fall ~

The divers who discovered the teenage girl's skeleton named her Naia (NY-uh) after an ancient Greek word for water goddesses. Naia was likely looking for water when she died. The Sac Actun cave system in Mexico's Yucatán Peninsula wasn't underwater when Naia was alive. In fact, the area was quite dry, with no lakes and rivers. Naia and the animals whose remains were found probably entered the caves seeking water and, in the darkness, fell to their death. When they stumbled upon the deep chamber, the divers named it Hoyo Negro, or "Black Hole."

Searching for the First Americans

Scientists studying early America are faced with solving a big puzzle: Who were the first Americans? Searching for when, how, and from where they entered and spread across the continent, **anthropologists** and archaeologists develop theories based on the evidence they discover. However, that evidence is scarce.

The earliest Americans had no writing system, so they didn't leave written records. They didn't build great buildings or monuments. Instead, archaeologists study stone tools and weapons and animal bones. Anthropologists uncover and examine human remains. Genetic scientists study DNA when it can be obtained from human remains. Together, they consider where the evidence was found and use scientific methods to date it. From this limited evidence, these scientists work toward the difficult task of discovering the first people in America—and their hidden history.

It may seem as if there's a lot of evidence about early humans, but it's all bits and pieces. It's challenging to build a meaningful, orderly account from this evidence.

~ Coming from Africa ~

Modern humans – *Homo sapiens* – first developed in Africa. All human skeletal remains in the Americas are *Homo sapiens*. More ancient forms of humans haven't been found. So when people came to the Americas, it was clearly part of the spread of modern humans out of Africa. They spread from there across Europe and Asia about 50,000 years ago. They reached what is today Europe about 45,000 years ago. They arrived at the areas that are now central Asia and Siberia about 40,000 years ago.

The People of Clovis

A road crew working near Clovis, New Mexico, accidentally made a huge discovery in 1932. They uncovered a pile of big ancient bones that belonged to extinct **mammoths**. Mixed among them were finger-long spearpoints. These spearpoints were evidence of what was once thought to be North America's first culture. Named the Clovis culture after the place, the culture appeared more than 13,000 years ago.

The spearpoints, now known as Clovis points, are the distinctive **artifacts** of the **culture**. They're made from fine, easily broken stone and have a lance-shaped tip and often extremely sharp edges. Shallow grooves, called flutes, run from the base toward the tip and may have helped attach the points to spear shafts. Clovis points have never been found anywhere except North America. They may be the first American invention!

Creating Clovis points required time and skill. These ones were found at a site in what is now the state of Iowa.

~ Making Tools ~

The Clovis people likely used a method called flint knapping to turn stone into weapons and tools. The action demands the ability to control how rocks break when struck. The best rocks to work with include flint, chert, jasper, and obsidian. Striking them with another rock or a piece of antler or bone breaks off a piece of rock called a flake. Flakes can be used as simple tools or further worked to create knives or scrapers. The core rock or a large flake can be turned into a spearpoint.

Evidence shows that the Clovis culture spread across most of North America. About 1,500 locations have been found to have evidence of the people being there. From animal bones found at the sites, we know the people hunted mammoths, mastodons, bison, deer, hares, reptiles, and amphibians. Some experts think the Clovis people hunted mammoths and mastodons so regularly that they may have played a part in the animals' extinction. The people also gathered plants to eat and may have fished as well.

Beyond that, we know little about the people who were part of the Clovis culture. We don't know what they looked like, how they dressed, or whether they built shelters. We don't know what their society was like. Whether they lived in family groups, had leaders, or followed a religion remains a mystery.

woolly mammoths

This man is looking at bison bones at a site in Oklahoma where a Clovis point was discovered.

~ Early, but Not First ~

It was long believed the people of the Clovis culture were the first to occupy the Americas. The culture was thought to have appeared about 13,600 years ago. However, recent studies of the evidence using advanced scientific methods have changed the dating. These studies show the culture first appeared between 13,200 and 13,100 years ago and disappeared about 12,900 years ago. No one knows for sure what caused the disappearance of the Clovis culture. Meanwhile, other evidence has emerged suggesting humans were in North America before the Clovis people.

Paisley Caves Discoveries

The same year divers found Naia's skeleton, archaeologists in Oregon made another important discovery. Working in the Paisley Caves, they uncovered human coprolites, or fossilized pieces of poop! Fossilized human waste may seem less exciting and important than a skeleton, but the scientists working with the archaeologists were able to get DNA from the coprolites. What they found changed people's thinking about North America's first people.

The DNA showed some of the coprolites were 14,400 years old. That meant there were people living in and around the Paisley Caves over 1,000 years before the Clovis culture appeared. The DNA also showed that, like Naia, these people were related to modern Native Americans. The discoveries made in the Paisley Caves meant that the long-held belief that the Clovis were the first people in North America was incorrect.

To the untrained eye, this may just look like a chunk of dried mud. An experienced archaeologist can recognize that it's a coprolite that can reveal important information about the past.

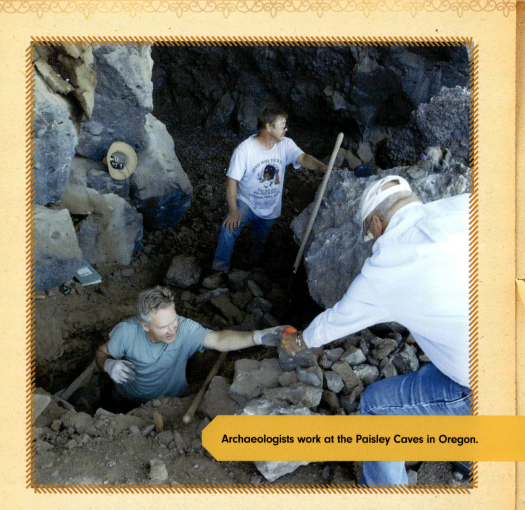

Archaeologists work at the Paisley Caves in Oregon.

~ More than Coprolites ~

Archaeologists found over 200 coprolites in the Paisley Caves, but the people who once occupied the Paisley Caves left behind much more than their fossilized waste. Archaeologists also found bits of rope, mats, and baskets. They also found wooden artifacts and **projectile** points. The projectile points differ from Clovis points, as they're narrower and lack flutes. In addition, archaeologists discovered **hearths** and the bones of animals such as waterfowl, fish, bison, horses, and mastodons. They even found bones of camels, which once roamed western North America.

Even Earlier People?

Some people think there is even more evidence, besides the discoveries from Oregon's Paisley Caves, of North American people before the Clovis culture. Some archaeologists and anthropologists believe they've found proof of people in Wisconsin, Pennsylvania, and Florida 14,000 to 16,000 years ago and in Kansas and Virginia about 20,000 years ago. There have even been claims for people in South Carolina 50,000 years ago!

However, not everyone is convinced the "evidence" from these locations can be trusted. It's not always easy to tell what's the work of humans. Natural processes can create rock fragments, or pieces, that resemble broken bits of man-made tools and weapons. Predators can leave marks on animal bones that resemble butchering by humans. People disagree on whether the "evidence" from these sites proves humans were there as early as some claim.

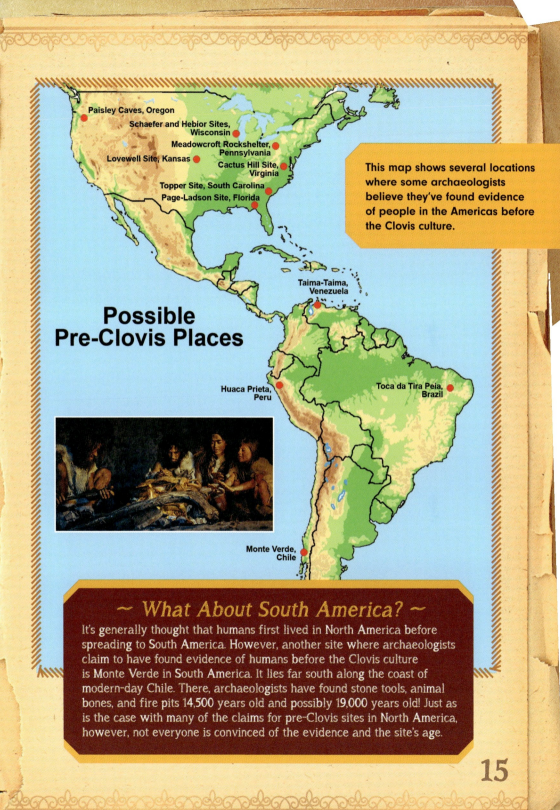

This map shows several locations where some archaeologists believe they've found evidence of people in the Americas before the Clovis culture.

Possible Pre-Clovis Places

~ What About South America? ~

It's generally thought that humans first lived in North America before spreading to South America. However, another site where archaeologists claim to have found evidence of humans before the Clovis culture is Monte Verde in South America. It lies far south along the coast of modern-day Chile. There, archaeologists have found stone tools, animal bones, and fire pits 14,500 years old and possibly 19,000 years old! Just as is the case with many of the claims for pre-Clovis sites in North America, however, not everyone is convinced of the evidence and the site's age.

Stumbling Across a Skull

Imagine going for a walk and finding a human skull. That's exactly what happened to two college students walking along the Columbia River in Kennewick, Washington, in 1996. They called the police, but it turned out there was no crime for them to investigate. The skull—and the rest of the skeleton that was found—belonged to a man who died about 9,000 years ago!

Scientists learn a lot by studying bones. They found out the Kennewick Man was about 5 feet 7 inches (1.7 m) tall, had well-developed muscles, and weighed about 160 pounds (73 kg). He was right-handed and around 40 years old when he died. He had broken ribs that never healed properly and other injuries, including a stone spearpoint in his hip bone.

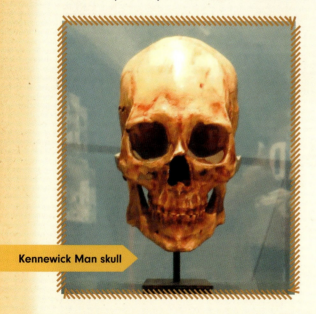
Kennewick Man skull

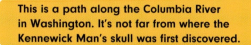

This is a path along the Columbia River in Washington. It's not far from where the Kennewick Man's skull was first discovered.

~ What Bones Reveal ~

By reading bones, scientists can learn what muscles a person used most. This is because muscles leave a mark where they attach to bones. The more a muscle is used, the stronger the mark. Kennewick Man's right arm and shoulder resemble a baseball pitcher's, suggesting not only that he was right-handed, but that he commonly made a throwing motion. His knee joints indicate he often squatted on his heels. His legs suggest he frequently waded in rapidly running shallow water. Chemical **analysis** of the bones showed that the Kennewick Man ate a lot of fish.

The Kennewick Man's bones, shown here, revealed much about his time on Earth.

The bones of the Kennewick Man revealed some clues about the society he lived in. From bone growth around the spearpoint in his hip bone, anthropologists know the injury happened when he was a teenager. They believe he survived only because he lived among people who took care of him. Those same people probably buried him after he died. Anthropologists know he was buried because his bones show no signs of gnawing or scavenging by animals.

The closest DNA match to Kennewick Man came from native peoples of the Northwest Coast, particularly the Colville people. They have long lived along the Columbia River where Kennewick Man was found. A member of the Colville Tribe is shown here with her child.

Early attempts to get DNA from Kennewick Man's bones failed. Anthropologists used the shape of his skull and bones to try to identify his closest living relatives, which they thought were **Polynesians** and Japan's Ainu people. However, they finally obtained DNA, which in 2015 showed that of peoples living today, Kennewick Man is most closely related to modern Native Americans.

~ The Rights to Kennewick Man ~

The Army Corps of Engineers manages the land where Kennewick Man was found. When the skeleton was found to be 9,000 years old, the corps ended scientific study and prepared to return it to local Native American groups who planned to rebury it as an ancestor. However, courts ruled the skeleton wasn't related to any living native people and scientists could study it. From 1998 to 2017, the remains were kept in a private location in a Washington museum. After the DNA findings, however, Kennewick Man was returned to Native Americans on February 17, 2017.

To the Native American tribes who claim him as an ancestor, Kennewick Man is known as "the Ancient One." After his return to the tribes, he was reburied according to their traditions.

Making the Way to America

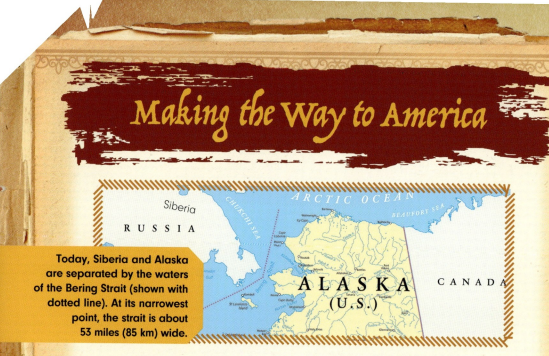

Today, Siberia and Alaska are separated by the waters of the Bering Strait (shown with dotted line). At its narrowest point, the strait is about 53 miles (85 km) wide.

The most supported theory about how people got to America says they crossed the Bering Land Bridge. This land once connected what's now Siberia, in northern Asia, to modern-day Alaska. Today, the Bering and the Chukchi Seas cover the land bridge. Thousands of years ago, however, the area was dry land. An ice age had lowered ocean levels by freezing much of Earth's water in massive ice sheets.

Modern humans reached northeastern Siberia about 30,000 years ago. DNA evidence shows that these early people, not others who came to the region later, were ancestors of Native Americans. They built settlements, and from there it wasn't far to the land bridge. However, about 25,000 years ago, Earth got colder. Results of this pushed Native Americans' ancestors out of northeastern Siberia.

Early people likely started the journey from Siberia to what is now North America about 25,000 years ago.

~ The Yana RHS Site ~

The oldest archaeological site in northeastern Siberia is called the Yana RHS site. At about 30,000 years old, it's twice as old as other known sites in the region. It's on the Yana River in Siberia's harsh Arctic region. The site was likely once a settlement. Archaeologists have found stone tools, items—such as hunting equipment and sewing tools—made of bone and ivory, and remains of animals such as reindeer, bison, and horses. They've also found decorated artifacts and objects meant to be worn as personal ornaments.

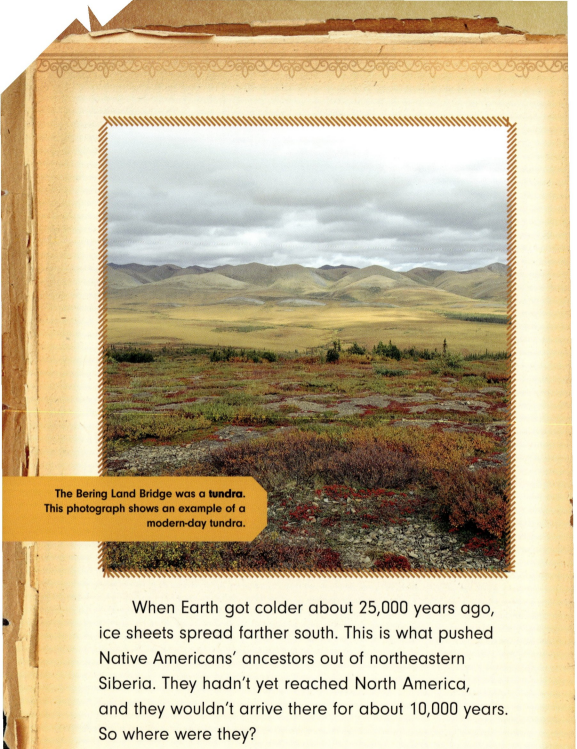

The Bering Land Bridge was a **tundra**. This photograph shows an example of a modern-day tundra.

When Earth got colder about 25,000 years ago, ice sheets spread farther south. This is what pushed Native Americans' ancestors out of northeastern Siberia. They hadn't yet reached North America, and they wouldn't arrive there for about 10,000 years. So where were they?

One **hypothesis** is that they lived on the Bering Land Bridge. It's based on the fact there are mutations, or changes, in the DNA of almost all Native Americans that don't appear in the existing remains of their Siberian ancestors. That means there had to be a population of ancestors cut off from the rest for thousands of years where these mutations could occur. It needed to be a place with animals to hunt and wood for fires. It needed to be close to North America too. That description could fit the Bering Land Bridge.

The land bridge wouldn't have supported huge animals like woolly mammoths, but smaller mammals likely lived there.

~ Life on the Land Bridge ~

Scientists have studied what the Bering Land Bridge was like at the time ancestors of modern Native Americans may have lived there. It was shrub tundra, dominated by dwarf shrubs such as willow and birch. Spruce trees might have grown in some protected places. It wasn't a place where you would have found woolly mammoths or bison. But it would have supported animals such as elk, bighorn sheep, and small mammals. The word "bridge" makes it sound as if it was narrow. However, it was likely about 600 miles (965 km) wide!

Crossing the Atlantic?

Some archaeologists think there might be a totally different way America's first people came to the land. They believe people belonging to the Solutrean (suh-LOO-tree-uhn) culture of Europe crossed the Atlantic Ocean to become the first people in North America. Archaeologists who think this base their theory on similarities between stone tools produced by the Solutrean and Clovis cultures.

According to the theory, the great ice sheets of the last ice age had forced the people of the Solutrean culture to Europe's Atlantic coast. They would have traveled north up the coast, then around the North Atlantic Ocean, taking advantage of an ice bridge that would have connected Europe and North America at the time. This theory is known as the North Atlantic Ice Edge Corridor Hypothesis. Most experts, however, don't think this hypothesis is very likely.

At first glance, a Solutrean point (left) may look somewhat like a Clovis point (right), but beyond both having a point, there aren't many similarities.

~ An Unlikely Hypothesis ~

Experts have objected to the North Atlantic Ice Edge Corridor Hypothesis, citing the fact that Solutrean and Clovis cultures seem to have been more different than similar. Clovis hunters didn't make use of marine resources. Solutrean hunters used shore and river resources. Most importantly, the Solutreans lived 5,000 years before the Clovis people. After the discovery of pre-Clovis sites, supporters of the hypothesis tried to link Solutreans to pre-Clovis people. However, not only did the Solutreans live earlier than the pre-Clovis people, but their stone tools also aren't very similar.

Recent Discoveries

Scientists have worked hard to learn about America's first peoples, but there are still more questions than answers. Discoveries keep being made, especially in the area of DNA.

Australasia, or Australia and its neighboring islands, is shown here.

~ Ancestors from Australia? ~

In 2015, a group of researchers published a study that examined the DNA of Native American populations in South America and Central America. They discovered Native Americans in Brazil's Amazon region had ancestors from Australasia, which is the name for Australia and its neighboring islands. No one is sure exactly how this relation happened. One possibility is that there was an Australasian population in northeastern Asia that mixed with Asian populations before they migrated to North America, and then eventually down to South America.

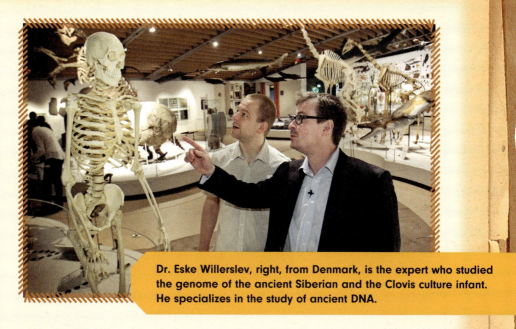

Dr. Eske Willerslev, right, from Denmark, is the expert who studied the genome of the ancient Siberian and the Clovis culture infant. He specializes in the study of ancient DNA.

In 2013, researchers mapped the genome of a Native American ancestor buried in southern Siberia about 24,000 years ago. They were surprised to discover he was European, not Asian! This meant even though the first people may have crossed the Bering Land Bridge from Asia, they may have carried European DNA.

Part of what keeps the history of North America's first people hidden is that the evidence often seems **contradictory**. A year after reporting on the European genome, the same expert mapped the genome of a 12,600-year-old infant of the Clovis culture. The infant had no European DNA and was found to have descended from ancient Asians.

In 2020, scientists suggested they had found evidence of humans in America nearly twice as long ago as was commonly thought. Nearly 2,000 stone artifacts were excavated at the Chiquihuite Cave in central Mexico. The scientists' study claimed the artifacts suggest people were living there 26,000 years ago. However, many experts don't think the "evidence" is enough to prove the claims. Evidence must be interpreted, and it's not always interpreted the same.

It should be clear by now how difficult it is to uncover the history of America's first peoples. Excavations help us learn a lot about the people who lived here long ago, but the findings don't always provide the answers we're searching for. Still, scientists are working every day to try to find answers. Perhaps in your lifetime we'll know for sure who the first Americans were!

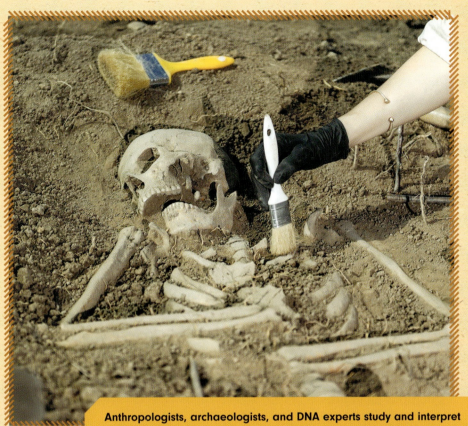

Anthropologists, archaeologists, and DNA experts study and interpret evidence as best they can. But future discoveries and scientific developments may change the way they view and interpret the evidence.

~ Yet Another Pre-Clovis Site? ~

A 2015 study reported on what's likely a pre-Clovis site near a river crossing in Canada. It's at least 13,300 years old and contains stone artifacts as well as horse and camel bones. Archaeologists believe ancient hunters attacked and butchered seven horses and one camel at the site. The date indicates a time before the Clovis culture. However, the stone artifacts don't provide enough information to identify the people.

While today there is a lot of evidence of people in America before the Clovis culture, much of this evidence is difficult even for experts to interpret.

GLOSSARY

analysis: the act or process of determining the ingredients that make up a substance

anthropologist: a person who studies humans and their ancestors through time and in relation to physical character, social relations, and culture

artifact: something made by humans in the past

contradictory: involving or having information that disagrees with other information

culture: the beliefs and ways of life of a group of people

DNA: part of the body that carries genetic information, which gives the instructions for life

hearth: a fire-hardened earth floor upon which ancient humans built fires

hypothesis: a proposed explanation of known facts that must be tested against facts discovered in the future to be proven

ice age: a period during which temperatures fall worldwide and large areas are covered with glaciers

mammoth: an extinct type of elephant of enormous size with long, upcurved tusks and well-developed body hair

Polynesian: someone native to the islands of the central and southern Pacific Ocean

projectile: capable of being hurled or thrown forward

tundra: cold northern lands that lack forests and have permanently frozen soil below the surface

Books

McNeese, Tim. *Native American America: North America Before 1492.* New York, NY: Rosen Publishing, 2021.

O'Brien, Cynthia. *Encyclopedia of American Indian History & Culture: Stories, Time Lines, Maps, and More.* Washington, DC: National Geographic, 2019.

Websites

10 Fascinating Facts About the First Americans
www.britannica.com/list/10-fascinating-facts-about-the-first-americans
Find out more interesting facts about the first Americans on this page.

Why Did the Clovis People Mysteriously Vanish?
www.history.com/news/clovis-migration-discovery
Learn more about the Clovis people here.

Publisher's note to educators and parents: *Our editors have carefully reviewed these websites to ensure that they are suitable for students. Many websites change frequently, however, and we cannot guarantee that a site's future contents will continue to meet our high standards of quality and educational value. Be advised that students should be closely supervised whenever they access the internet.*

INDEX

Bering Land Bridge 20, 22, 23, 27

Chiquihuile Cave 28

Clovis 8, 9, 10, 11, 12, 14, 15, 24, 25, 27, 29

Colville Tribe 18

coprolites 12, 13

Homo sapiens 7

Kennewick Man 16, 17, 18, 19

Monte Verde 15

Naia 5, 12

North Atlantic Ice Edge Corridor Hypothesis 25

Paisley Caves 12, 13, 14

Solutrean culture 24, 25

spearpoints 8, 9, 16, 18, 25

Willerslev, Eske 27

Yana RHS site 21